Charmaine Vincent is a passionate, award-winning female entrepreneur. Charmaine has experienced loss and success in equal measure. She's encountered incredible business accomplishments, millionaire status and multiple national award wins. But she has also confronted loss, shame, divorce, gender inequality and vulnerability in abundance.

She fully recognises her need, not want, to make a difference to others and be a positive role model for her daughter: a powerful woman with an inner girl's voice who isn't afraid of showing vulnerability.

Her mission is simple: to empower others to become the best version of themselves by showing up authentically, with no apologies.

For my beautiful daughter, Florence. Thank you for giving me purpose in life, for showing me what real love is, for making me a kinder person, and for inspiring me to be the courageous woman I am today.

Charmaine Vincent

Authentically You, with No Apologies!

Why Vulnerability is Your Ultimate Superpower in Leadership, Love and Life

Austin Macauley Publishers

London * Cambridge * New York * Sharjah

A CIP catalogue record for this title is available from the British Library.

ISBN 9781035863914 (Paperback)
ISBN 9781035863938 (ePub e-book)
ISBN 9781035863921 (Audiobook)

www.austinmacauley.com

First Published 2025
Austin Macauley Publishers Ltd®
1 Canada Square
Canary Wharf
London
E14 5AA

Table of Contents

Intro: This is Me   **11**

  Owning My Story   *11*

Chapter 1: Holding the Mirror Up   **20**

  Staring Vulnerability in the FACE!   *20*

  Staring Vulnerability in the F.A.C.E   *33*

Chapter 2: Ghosts of the Past   **35**

  When Your History Attempts to Hijack Your Present   *35*

Chapter 3: You are What You Value   **48**

  Aligning Your Behaviours with Your Values   *48*

Chapter 4: Goal Setting with Your Heart   **59**

  Chasing Feelings, Not Numbers   *59*

Chapter 5: Owning Your New Superpowers!   **68**

  Cut the Cord and Wear the Cape   *68*

Five Step Framework

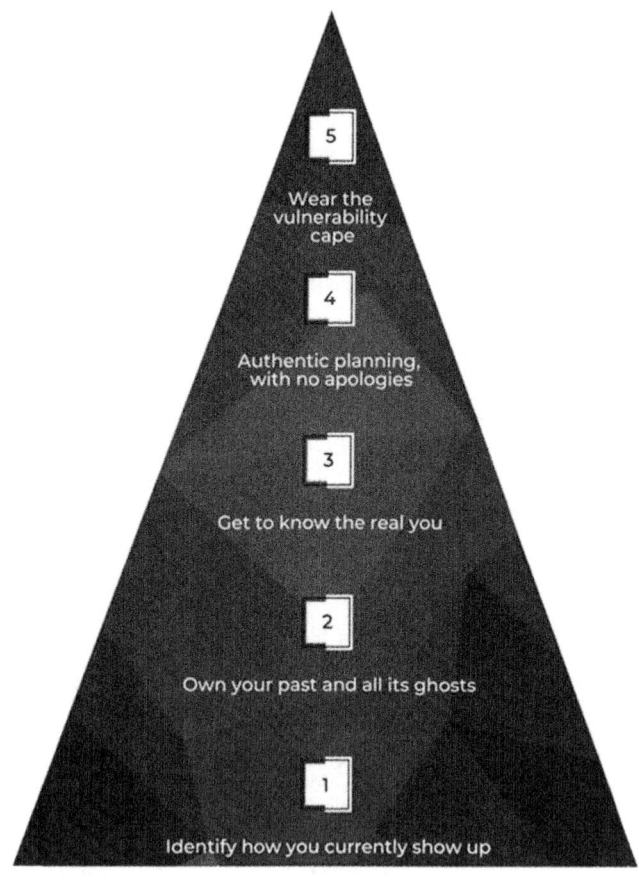

5

Wear the
vulnerability
cape

4

Authentic planning,
with no apologies

3

Get to know the real you

2

Own your past and all its ghosts

1

Identify how you currently show up

"Why Vulnerability is Your Ultimate Superpower in Leadership, Love & Life"

By Charmaine Vincent

Intro
This is Me

Owning My Story

Have you ever wondered why, on an aeroplane, they tell you to put your own oxygen mask on before helping a child put theirs on? The concept feels crazy, doesn't it? Most of us will instinctively want to protect. You'll probably believe that putting a child's mask on first is absolutely the right thing to do.

The reality is, if you don't take care of yourself, you can't take care of others, even those you love the most. The moment we make self-care a priority, is the moment we inherit 20:20 vision. Now, I'll let you into the world's best kept secret: the exact same concept applies in leadership and love. The relationships you build are dictated by the person that shows up in that hour, day, month, year. The real you, with no mask and a bucket load of authenticity and vulnerability. You will inevitably attract a different, more meaningful relationship if you allow your authentic self to shine through. Let me give you an example; most of us have probably experienced poor leadership, aggressive bosses, that draconian leader even, who ultimately followed in someone else's footsteps. The chances are they've been shown the ropes by someone possessing all the wrong values and their actions and behaviours are ultimately that of someone that leads with fear as opposed to their heart. Poor values and questionable leadership techniques are typically inherited from other leaders, and it's this type of benchmarking that can cause a Mexican wave of destruction. To that end, it's not really their fault. Decades of living in a Patriarchal society arguably hasn't helped. Strong leadership should be about putting your people first and coaching them to become the best version of themselves.

If you don't show up as your authentic self, remove the mask, ditch the old school 80s corporate leader approach and show vulnerability, how do you expect to get the most out of your people? How will they respect you? And most importantly, who is giving them permission to be 100% themselves and shine authentically with no apologies?

"Only when we know our own darkness well, can we be present with the darkness of others."

Brene Brown

Matters of the heart are ultimately the same. Turning 40 years old, with two failed marriages in my locker and 13 years of therapy later, meant, I finally knew who I was. I used to be afraid of showing up as the 'real me' and was absolutely petrified of being judged by others. Now I'm unapologetically me. I live by my values, I wear my heart on my sleeve and above all, I know what makes me shine. This enables me to be a good friend, mother, emotional partner, and an authentic leader that inspires others to recognise their strengths and be the best version of themselves.

Okay, so that's easy for me to say after years of soul searching and coaching. I guess the real question is, what ultimately holds us back? What prevents us from showing up as our authentic selves to begin with? Lack of confidence, fear of being judged, perhaps? Now this is where our mindset will always play such an important role.

Take a second to try and imagine a world where we weren't consumed about what others think. Free from judgment around our leadership style, our parenting techniques, our choice of clothing, the friends we pick, even. Here's the bad news, we are all HUGE judges, it's human nature and ultimately our biggest internal saboteur. Perhaps the solution isn't necessarily fantasising about a world where people aren't judging you. Perhaps, it's more about, you, NOT JUDGING YOU.

Let's be honest, judging ourselves and lack of self-care and kindness is arguably at the root of all our problems. Feeling empowered to lead and love with your heart and showing vulnerability by choosing courage over comfort, is literally game changing. The ultimate key to success isn't about bench marking against others. Okay, sure, it's healthy to align with other people's values and to appreciate their contributions, but great things only happen when you get comfortable with what you see in the mirror.

If you're in a constant state of judgment, the chances are you're operating below the line as a leader, a parent, a partner, even. There's also a high probability that you, like so many, have experienced the crippling feeling of Imposter Syndrome. It can be completely debilitating and there remains a lot of confusion about what this means and how to approach it.

So, if you're reading this now, thinking, *Yep, this is 100% me,* know that you're not alone and you're simply bang in the middle of a challenging chapter in your own story. Thankfully you have the pen. You're the author and completely in charge of when you add a full stop, turn the page, and begin a brand-new chapter. One full of glitter, hope, authenticity, vulnerability, and love.

Now I've shared a few words of wisdom, I guess I should formally introduce myself.

I'm Charmaine Vincent, an award-winning female entrepreneur, a mother, a friend and guru to many, mentor, business coach, charity ambassador and all-round chief juggler. I wear a multitude of hats but honestly wouldn't have it any other way. After years of harnessing an overwhelming feeling of inadequacy, born from feeling rejected and unheard in childhood and a male dominated board room, I had one of those eureka moments. The kind that finally made me realise that being my authentic self, was way more powerful than trying to fit in. I realised that I didn't need to pretend, and I certainly wasn't prepared to sacrifice who I really was, the real me! I finally stopped apologising for caring. Caring about making a difference, about being true to my values, about showing my vulnerability and being honest about my vision. I can't tell you how incredible that felt.

I'm a true believer that our childhood can play a significant role in our future. Take a moment and imagine your childhood as a blockbuster movie. What name would you give it? Can you imagine the trailer? Every movie is made up of actors and actresses. They all have different roles to play. Some have leading roles, whilst others have more of a cameo appearance. Here's the thing. The decision around leading roles, cameo appearances and how many lines are distributed to those characters in your future, sit firmly in your hands. What I mean by that, is, how much emotional baggage we allow ourselves to carry forward is ultimately a choice. We can't change the past, that's a fact.

We need to be willing to acknowledge that some wounds may never fully heal, and that's also okay. We need to be courageous enough to move towards the pain and get comfortable with being uncomfortable. Only then can our superpowers genuinely work their magic in our present, and let's be honest, that's absolutely where it counts.

My childhood was like so many others. An 80s child, growing up in a council house, fully equipped with that classic olive bathtub, vintage record player audio tower and a fabulous pair of Fisher Price roller-skates. Our childhood home was in a small grove with a community of neighbours that regularly chatted over their garden gates with a cup of coffee and would implicitly trust each other to babysit each other's kids. We were such a cliché; we even had my grandmother living literally next door.

I'm happy to admit, I wasn't very academic, I was more creative. I got so much joy from drawing, painting, creative play and had a brilliant imagination. My mother was a nurturer. She was and still is one of the kindest people I know. We had very little money growing up, but what we lacked on one hand, was more than made up for with a comforting smile and a reassuring hug. I have huge admiration for my beautiful mother. Her and my father split when I was only 4 years old. I watched her juggling two jobs trying to make ends meet for myself and my two sisters. I have very vivid early memories of seeing my mum struggling and displaying vulnerability.

You soon realise there are some things you can't unsee, unhear or fix. There is no magic wand, and there is no time machine.

I left home at the young age of 16. A volatile relationship with my stepdad unintentionally created an independent young woman that wanted to find her wings and stand on her on two feet. Whilst I've spent years in therapy discussing the rejection I felt from someone that should have instinctively supported and protected me, I can now reflect and feel grateful for the fire in the belly I now have as a result of that situation.

My path wasn't a conventional one, there was no college, no university, no money, and no support. Now, I don't want to create a bleak, tragic picture here, and I certainly don't want you to get that tiny violin out on my behalf. I mention this because that aside, I was okay. I had stuff that money simply couldn't buy. I had spirit, big dreams, and one hell of an incredible human by my side, my sister. My older sister, Celestine, was a real-life superhero. She was only two years older than me but somehow managed to scoop me up and make me feel loved and empowered to be me. Sometimes, you need someone to hold your hand initially to truly believe what is possible.

There was a time I was riddled with shame about my lack of education and my roots. I'd compare myself to others and dread being asked, where I went to university. Thankfully this is not how I feel today. It's part of me, my story is unique and I'm proud of how I've coped with all my chapters, especially those I've had very little control over.

Okay, let's fast forward to present day. I now have two babies. My beautiful daughter Florence and my work baby, my recruitment business, Baltimore Consulting. Both have made me feel extremely vulnerable at different stages. I've experienced Imposter Syndrome and asked myself the question that most parents and entrepreneurs have asked themselves at some point, "Am I good enough?" I now know the answer is always categorically yes, but that doesn't mean the journey hasn't taken me to some dark places along the way.

There's no real right or wrong, nor is there a definitive rule book. I now unapologetically listen to how I feel. The most amazing guiding signal of your life is how you feel. What I now know is that helping others and watching them flourish is what makes me shine.

My daughter made me a better, kinder, more fulfilled person and ultimately gave me the strength to turn my dreams into reality. My company unsurprisingly has real purpose, strong values, and real heart at the very core of it. We specialise in placing niche and senior skills into vulnerable subject areas within the public sector. Okay, so it's not exciting tech and there are no sexy marketing strategies, but here's the thing. We make a difference to the community, we put our people first and wait for it...we make a profit doing so. Despite being told for many years, by industry leaders (sadly all male), that if I combine all the above without being cutthroat, I will undoubtedly fail. Guess what? I think being the proud owner of a 30 million turnover SME heading into its 12th year of trading is proof enough that being authentic and leading with your heart, can yield more purposeful results, without cutting corners.

That's the kind of stuff that helps me sleep at night. It's the reason I can shine unapologetically about what I do.

I spend most days genuinely wanting to change the world and help others, it's in my make-up, my DNA even, I sometimes think spiritually it was my calling card and ultimately why I've been gifted the life I have today.

I can talk from experience now. I've had my heart broken many times, but I know how euphoric it feels to fall in love. I've been divorced twice, but I feel proud that I gave my heart fully to enter marriage in the first place. I've lost a dear friend to cancer, but I'm thankful that my mother and an ex-husband survived the big C. I know the excruciating pain of losing a child, but I am grateful for the unconditional love I felt immediately after giving birth to my incredible daughter. I failed my driving test, but then passed because I wasn't willing to give up. I've got myself into debt more times than I care to remember, but I am now a millionaire, because anything other than dreaming big and reaching for the stars was and will never be an option for me.

My long-winded point being, we need to remember that our failures shape our successes. When we fail, we learn and when we learn, we grow. I've failed many times in my life, both professionally and personally but I've never stopped learning and I'm comfortable being vulnerable. I wear my heart on my sleeve, but I make bold, brave decisions that not only change my life, but those around me. I'm confident but emotional, brave but occasionally fearful! But the one thing I never waiver from now is self-belief. There will always be a queue of people to tell you, you're not good enough, that now isn't the right time to set up your own business, that your parenting skills are less than perfect.

The reality is, if you choose to back yourself 100%, and believe that anything is possible, only great things will follow.

Show up with the right mindset, listen and learn from the best and be willing to take massive action to change your life.

Showing vulnerability is your ultimate superpower, that's a FACT–You just need to get comfortable with being your authentic self. That's the challenge. The question is, are you ready to embark on that journey?

I promise, it will change your life!

Chapter 1
Holding the Mirror Up

Staring Vulnerability in the FACE!

"The only impossible journey is the one you never begin."

Tony Robbins

When was the last time you looked in the mirror and loved what you saw? I mean, genuinely loved the person staring back at you. I'm talking physically, emotionally, and mentally. The whole person! Do you love the values you hold, the contributions you make, the passion you display? Is it possible you've never actually taken the time to look? How crazy does that sound when you say it out loud. We're all creatures of habit, to a point. We walk past the mirror literally every day. We brush our teeth, do our hair, get dressed, but admiring or judging your own physicality is such surface level viewing. Investing the time to lift the bonnet and get to know the real you, to accept the authentic person staring back, is a real game changer.

Now, before investing in others, be it professionally, personally, or romantically, you need to you get comfortable with yourself. Learning to love the person you see staring back is almost as important as the air that you breathe. I know, it sounds so dramatic, but it's 100% true.

A big part of this will come from how emotionally intelligent you are, or in-fact aspire to be. Step 1 unsurprisingly is self-awareness. So many of us love the idea of being self-aware and have probably boasted to family, friends, colleagues, staff that it's a superpower we hold. The reality is, being self-aware means, we acknowledge our strengths, our flaws, our emotional triggers, our insecurities, and we absolutely know how and when they manifest themselves. Alarmingly only 10–15% of the population are fully self-aware. I think this comes back down to aspirations versus investing the time to lift the bonnet and get comfortable with being uncomfortable.

I remember going to the funfair as a child and being completely freaked out by those weird mirrors. Instead of a normal plain mirror that reflects a perfect mirror image, these mirrors reflect a distorted image, one that isn't true or authentic. When you choose to live a life that is restricted and masked, you're effectively hanging one of these carnival mirrors up in your home, place of work, even in your relationships.

Exercise

Let's try something. Put down this book and find the nearest mirror. Use the camera on your phone if you don't have one close by.

It's important that you allow yourself 60 seconds of uninterrupted observations of the beautiful person staring back. This might feel strange. In fact, it should.

You may even be asking yourself: "Will these next 60 seconds, make me feel vulnerable?" Well, the answer is YES, 100%, but that's why you're here, right? Great things happen when you step out of your comfort zone.

It's time to get comfortable, being uncomfortable. It's step one for you on that self-investment journey.

Say what you see; brave, sad, courageous, hardworking, tired etc. There's no right or wrong, this is your self-portrait, you are truly unique.

Take 60 seconds now

How did it make you feel?

....

....

....

....

....

What do you see?

....

....

....

....

....

Have you learnt anything about yourself?

....

....

....

....

....

....

....

A big part of this journey is changing the dialogue in your own head.

Some of us may live in a very victim, persecuting mentality whereby regardless of facts and truth, the glass is always half empty and life is happening to you, not for you. Whilst others will live their life with curiosity and a growth mind-set; they will be open to possibilities and change, have a coaching mentality, and always strive for the why and the how. It's less about where you are today and more about recognising where you typically default and how this may impact. Ask yourself this: "Am I happy with where I am?" Don't forget, you're the author in your story, only you can change the chapter.

Different people, scenarios and environments will hold different levels of vulnerability. There's a cycle and when you start to understand where you are and why, you can then decide to act on becoming more accepting and more curious about evolving into the authentic person you're supposed be. With NO apologies!

Imagine if you walked into a room and were faced with two magic mirrors. One full of shadows and fear, and the other of light and curiosity.

Which are you drawn to? Which one would you pick when you stare vulnerability in the face? Maybe you feel powerless and find yourself defaulting unintentionally to the shadows. The good news is, we can all move from the shadows to the light, you'll just need to get that superpower cape on first.

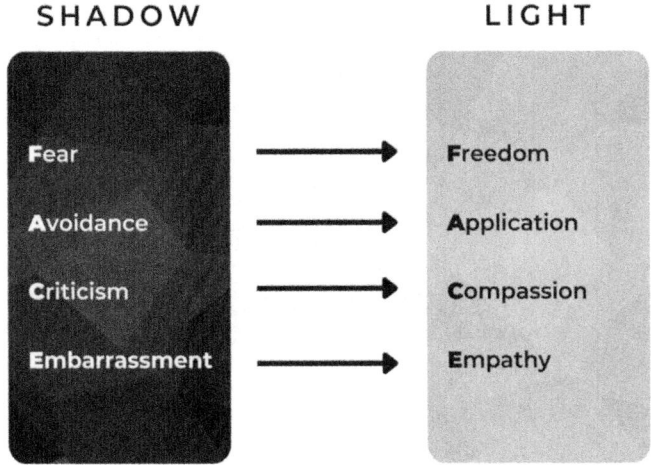

SHADOW   LIGHT

SHADOW	LIGHT
Fear	Freedom
Avoidance	Application
Criticism	Compassion
Embarrassment	Empathy

The vulnerability cycle should act as your mirror. You will almost certainly be at different stages of vulnerability in different areas of your life too.

Leadership, partners, friends, and parenting could force you into a different stage. The question is, why is this even important to know?

Professor and author, Brené Brown, suggests that vulnerability is an important measure of courage, and that it allows us to be seen and understood by the people who are important in our lives. Being vulnerable also serves as an important way to foster authenticity, belongingness, and love.

It's so important that you have the tools to move from the shadows of vulnerability, into the light where you will inevitably shine as a leader and partner.

Stage 1 Turning Fear into Freedom

So why do people often fear vulnerability? The fear of vulnerability is also often related to a fear of rejection or abandonment. Fear could show up before an interview, ahead of a promotion, before a date, on your wedding day, even. The very thought of showing others that you're vulnerable, will feel crippling.

It's important to understand if you're genuinely scared of being vulnerable.

Let's quickly break down the signs:

- You find yourself caring more about portraying 'the right' image to the world than being your true, authentic self and showing your true feelings.
- You get annoyed and start fights and disagreements over small things when you feel vulnerable.

- You're closed off from talking and resentful at the request.
- You always have one foot out the door ready to leave and find it hard to be present.

When I set up my business, I had a major fear of vulnerability; I didn't even realise how deep and big that fear was at the time, and more importantly, how it was holding me back as a leader and a partner. I had no idea how much that fear influenced my thoughts and behaviour. I was self-sabotaging so many areas of my life, especially my relationship with men. I wasn't even aware of it. The most confusing thing was, I did trust my partner. I trusted him with everything; the problem was I didn't trust myself to be fully open, on the off-chance I would be judged, rejected, or hurt. Old wounds prevented me from showing up authentically and it was such a lonely place to be.

Childhood abandonment meant I felt like I wasn't deserving of love, I believed I would be hurt in the end anyway, and so I closed parts of myself off to protect and shield from future disappointment. I say all of this because I've done a complete 360 in a decade. Yes, it's taken me ten years to create secure attachment with others.

I now assume that I am loveable, kind and ultimately deserve to be loved. I'm comfortable with vulnerability and showing up as me. It didn't happen overnight, but the journey has been 100% worth it.

The truth is, no relationship, no matter how healthy or strong it is, can survive without vulnerability. For a relationship to truly work and flourish, both parties need to be willing to open themselves up to one another completely, even though there's a possibility they may get hurt in the end. The same applies in leadership, open honest dialogue is how we grow. We need to be willing to give and receive feedback and learn the power of 'pause'.

I now coach others on the power of vulnerability and fully embrace my authentic self, along with all the chapters of my story. This shift of mindset increases self-belief and enables me to not take other people's judgment to heart.

Showing up authentically and honestly, will lead to freedom. It's important to know that fear and freedom battle with each other on a regular basis. In one hour, you could go from complete freedom to fear, withdrawn and isolated all off the back of a comment from someone that isn't aligned with your thoughts and values. You have the power to stop fighting and fearing. Simply put down your sword and exit the battle circle. It's empowering, believe me. When you stop fighting and remove any personal shame around how you feel and how you show up, freedom is inevitable.

Stage 2 Turning Avoidance into Application

Insecurity is present in all of us, and it's so strong that we often go out of our way to avoid situations that might make us feel fragile. Brene Brown famously described the ways we try to sidestep the shaky feeling of vulnerability. We emotionally 'armour up' each morning when we face the day to avoid feeling shame, anxiety, uncertainty, and fear. When avoidance is in full swing, there's a constant feeling of dread and you probably find yourself consistently imagining all the way that things could go wrong. You have little trust in others, you avoid getting too close to avoid being hurt and ultimately pull away from vulnerable people if they attempt to get too close. Ultimately an avoider's friendships and relationships are low effort and low reward but it's unlikely you'd tell yourself this.

This.

The dialogue is likely to be that of someone in denial. If this doesn't sound like you, there's a high chance you'll have people in your life that fall into that avoidance category.

Internalising what other people think about us can also make perfect soil for our negative thoughts to flourish. Which in turn means we are seeing ourselves as flawed or imperfect which nudges us to distance from other people and avoid vulnerability.

Common signs of avoidance are:

- We don't ask for what we need.
- We deny problems rather than confronting them.
- We don't speak our truth.
- We shut down, isolate, or leave rather than talking things out.
- We use hypervigilance as a tool to maintain our people-pleasing.
- We avoid intimacy.

The question is how do you remove the shame, start moving forward towards people and situations that will make you vulnerable and force you to hold the mirror up and get comfortable with the truth? It must start with taking positive steps alone, with no audience.

Know your triggers, practice self-compassion and be gentle with yourself when you make mistakes. Only once you give yourself permission to make mistakes and get comfortable with being uncomfortable, can you then apply yourself and connect with others who share your values and support your growth. Avoiding vulnerability won't make those feelings disappear. In fact, it enhances that feeling of anxiety. Taking brave, bold steps forward and pushing out of your comfort zone is the application needed to hold the mirror up and start getting comfortable.

Stage 3: Turning Criticism into Compassion

"My stomach looks so bulky," "I'm not good enough for that promotion," "I'll probably never find someone that we love me, the way I am."

We frequently hear people verbalise these types of self-critiques to their friends, families and even strangers online. In such a hyper-connected, self-obsessed society, this tendency toward judgment can be hard to escape, especially for women. It was suggested that 60% of adult women have negative thoughts about themselves on a weekly basis. This statistic is devastating but true and certainly resonates with me.

Under distress, this self-criticism heightens and when times get tough and people become upset, we typically default to self-criticism.

Having self-compassion has profound effects both internally and externally. Even showing compassion to others can't be achieved unless you have compassion for yourself. The same rules apply, it must start with you, and you must put the effort into getting to know the real you, without the unhelpful critic and judgement to really know what compassion feels like.

Many of us are more comfortable providing help and compassion to others than we are receiving it for ourselves, but self-criticism will always subconsciously cripple these efforts. Keeping a kindness/compassion diary is a positive step forward. I think the 60 second rule is so powerful. Accept that you may not be able to stop that critic showing up, but only give it 60 seconds. Hear it and then kill it with kindness. In that very moment, find compassion for yourself and write down a quality, a strength, a moment in the day you have demonstrated kindness to others. Celebrate you, offer compassion and slowly the noise of the critic will become quieter and less frequent.

Stage 4: Turning Embarrassment into Empathy

This truth is, so many of us struggle to believe with absolute certainty in our full potential and it's the shame connected to our roots and experiences that seem to restrict our ability to see the wood through the trees.

This naturally has a direct impact on the action we're willing to take, to achieve our goals, which in turn impacts the results we do or do not achieve.

Think about it; if you lack self-belief, there's no way you will allow yourself to see your full potential. And if you don't see your full potential, there's a high probability you won't act, and if you don't act, goals, dreams, careers milestones and any other type of result becomes simply unobtainable. So, it must start with positive mind-set and self-belief–This is something you can't compromise on.

There are so many reasons for shame and embarrassment, and these are sadly triggered by childhood or early memories and experiences. The school we attended, our family roots, our lack of education, previous infidelity, or relationship breakdown etc.

When we start getting comfortable with celebrating differences in ourselves and others and turning the page on chapters that we now have very little control on, only then can we start to display empathy and kindness to the child that lives in every single one of us.

Take a second to think about a moment in your life that caused you embarrassment. Maybe it was at school, a social gathering, in the workplace even. Regardless of where it was, now vision your younger self standing there. Imagine you're embarrassed and crying. As an adult what words of kindness would you offer that child. Would you empathise with them? Would you wipe their tears and reassure them that they are good enough and encourage them to love who they are?

The point here is, the concept of a child displaying vulnerability, will probably make most of us offer compassion and empathy. If we remember that there is an inner child in every single one of us that needs that same level of love, it may just help us move from embarrassment to empathy.

Don't just think it, take massive action, and own it. Dreams only come true if you believe it's possible and act. Fairy steps are okay if you're moving forward.

There's been so many turning points in my life and had I not believed in my full potential and removed the shame and embarrassment attached to my past and how I show up, I simply wouldn't be where I am today.

I wouldn't be shining unapologetically and, I certainly wouldn't be writing this book.

Exercise

Staring Vulnerability in the F.A.C.E

Take a moment to consider how you show up at work, in your relationships and socially.

Are there differences?

Do certain people or situations make you feel more vulnerable than others?

Knowing with absolute certainty how you show up and how you feel when staring vulnerability in the face, will ultimately help you grow.

The mirror is your friend.

It's genuinely game changing to understand if you gravitate towards the shadows or the light in different areas of your life. For example, you may feel complete freedom at work, having invested in your career for the past 20 years and be comfortable showing vulnerability. However, following heartbreak and divorce, now find yourself in a classic avoidant space when it comes to any relationship to avoid getting hurt.

There are no rules with this task; it's simply about recognising where you are today and deciding if you want to change tomorrow.

Label it and OWN it!

F	**Fear vs Freedom**
A	**Avoidance vs Action**
C	**Criticism vs Compassion**
E	**Embarrassment vs Empathy**

PRESENT

Work

Relationship

Socially

FUTURE

Work

Relationship

Socially

Chapter 2
Ghosts of the Past

When Your History Attempts to Hijack Your Present

"I Am Not What Happened To Me; I Am What I Choose To Become."

Nelson Mandela

At what age do we truly know ourselves? The truth is, there is no hard, fast rule for this. I've spent years being fascinated by the psychology of people and how we have the power to make or break our future. 13 years on from investing in therapists, psychotherapists, executive coaches etc. and I still get those light bulb moments that positively change how I parent, lead, and love. Whilst age is but a number in my opinion, I do believe that time, curiosity, and the willingness to listen, can make the perfect potion for tackling whatever life throws at you.

We've all heard that saying 'ghosts of the past', but how many of us truly recognise our own ghosts?

When you think about the fact that we've grown up with Disney movies that always finish with that happily ever after line, there's no surprise that so many of us inherit unrealistic expectations over what happiness should look like.

You can spend a lifetime comparing to others. Their lives, their bodies, their jobs, their kids, their partners.

Let's be honest, social media now has a big part to play in the filtered, unrealistic, unobtainable world in which we see. Social media provides a mask for others to hide behind and a platform to create 'the perfect picture' of what life should look like. It's the shame and inadequacy that follows from feeling like you're not keeping up with the Jones's or you don't have that 'polished, perfect life'. This can prevent you from showing up, authentically, with no apologies. It can be all consuming and immensely crippling.

There's no real surprise that so many of us default to putting our ghosts in a box. We somehow think that by closing the lid, they will disappear, and we can move on with our lives. The reality is, that box isn't airtight, and it will almost definitely open all by itself. Those ghosts will make themselves known, normally when you least expect it, want it, or need it. There's no masking tape or gorilla glue strong enough to keep them in.

We must go on a courageous journey that will force us to be vulnerable again. Some say, we need to go backwards before we can move forward. Effectively moving towards the pain will enable the healing process to begin. For those ghosts to truly R.I.P and for you to make a conscious decision to exit that crazy metaphoric roller-coaster that you've been riding, unknowingly, for your entire life!

You've got to get that cape back on and open the box.

No one is exempt from these rules. Facing those demons head on, will prevent our history from hijacking our present and these are the 3 steps needed, to enable your ghosts to R.I.P.

Step 1 Recognise your triggers

Part of the self-awareness journey is recognising when you're triggered. Sounds easy, but so many of us are oblivious to this. How many times have you turned to a friend or family member for advice, wholeheartedly believing you're in a perfectly reasonable state of mind and fully expecting them to agree with all your laboured points. Only to then find out, that in their opinion, you're being completely irrational and hot headed because something or someone has triggered you.

Here's the thing. We completely trust the judgement of a friend and would be willing to hold the mirror up if they suggest you need to, but until that point, alarmingly, we are completely blind-sided by our emotions.

It's a journey of self-discovery. A great way to start to recognise when you're being triggered, is to understand what attachment style you are. Attachment theory refers to a set of ideas formulated by psychologists in the 1960s that give us a useful guide to how we behave in relationships. Knowing whether we are secure, anxious, or avoidant in our attachment patterns gives us a vocabulary with which to get on top of some very tricky dynamics and helps us grow into more predictable and more joyful humans.

Love and affirmation can literally blow into your life at any second, and if you're not securely attached, you won't be willing to receive it.

A secure person may spot when they're being triggered, but without the self-investment, self-awareness, and willingness to get to know yourself, you will be completely oblivious and possibly resentful to the suggestion when sensitive feedback is offered.

How can someone remotely offer you feedback and advice around your actions and behaviour, if you're not even curious enough to get to know yourself in the first place? Makes sense, right? It's worth flagging that your past, present, and future attachment styles can, and probably will vary. Again, you're very much in the driving seat for this.

The three most recognised attachment styles are:

- Secure
- Anxious
- Avoidant

So, you might be thinking, what do attachment styles have to do with emotional triggers? Well, the answer is, absolutely everything. If you're someone with a secure attachment style, you'll assume that you are loveable, and you deserve to be loved. You'll typically be comfortable with vulnerability and showing up as your true authentic self. This in turn means, you should recognise when you're emotionally triggered and act accordingly. Being secure doesn't make you exempt from vulnerability; far from it. You just have more tools in your box, you accept boundaries and won't push others. You won't mind being vulnerable and will address directly but not confrontationally.

If you're secure, the chances are your relationships as a leader and a partner will be much stronger. Securely attached people are attracted to securely attached people. From a coaching perspective, it's not about being right. It's about finding the appropriate evidence that others can template which will then ultimately encourage change.

Alternatively, you could be anxious. An anxious attachment style will epitomise that fear of abandonment. You will see rejection when it's not occurring: a friend could be tired and rain check on your dinner date, however, you will see it as them rejecting you and sadly won't consider other circumstances.

You immediately jump to taking it all very personally and are quick to right people off. This in turn means that feedback as a leader and partner, will feel difficult for everyone involved. You will unintentionally make situations difficult when triggered.

You won't be receptive to understanding how to grow and could even be described as passive aggressive in conflict. Less flexible and more controlling!

Common signs could be:

- Almost willing to give up yourself to make others happy due to your overwhelming fear of abandonment.
- Agree to things with others but then resent them, for what is ultimately your lack of honesty and communication.
- Attracted to relationships with people that need work.
- You'll see a new relationship as a project, incomplete and gravitate towards someone you could add value to.
- You'll remember things more negatively than what they were and the narrative you tell yourself and others will be fuelled with negativity.

Finally, the Avoidant. A secure person will run for the hills and an anxious person will want to fix you. The most dangerous part of being an avoidant leader or lover is if you're completely unaware of your avoidant style and ultimately refuse to recognise your triggers. Building relationships will be tough and you will ultimately cause a professional and personal blocker, due to lack of trust for others.

The moment people get close, you push them away as you believe they will hurt you. You'll be more likely to end friendships and pull away from more vulnerable people if you feel they're getting too close. Due to a distinct lack of emotion, an avoidant will struggle with vulnerability and will carry a feeling of being disconnection from others.

Common signs could be:

- Never allow themselves to be vulnerable.
- Not emotionally available.
- Carries a lot of shame but won't freely admit it.
- Minimal effort into any relationship.
- Conversation doesn't go as deep.
- Feeling of discomfort when you're in the company of someone that encourages you to acknowledge your wounds.
- Emotionally overwhelmed to even look at patterns and historical trends.

Our attachment style can ultimately impact how we give and receive love and how we build healthy relationship with others. They form a big part of understanding when we're triggered, so, making this a priority in our self-investment journey, is critical.

Step 2 Identify Your Ghost(s)

I mentioned in my introduction, that a volatile relationship with my stepdad during childhood went on to have a huge impact later in life. The truth is, even now, as a woman in her early 40s that feels she finally got her shit together, the trauma from my childhood and that deep rooted feeling of abandonment and rejection still occasionally rears its ugly head.

The difference is now, my resilience and bounce back ability is significantly better than what it ever was. I know when I feel triggered, and I've decided to stop letting the ghosts of my past impact my present.

So, what does that even mean? It means again, we have a choice. I identified my ghosts and whilst I'm not suggesting it was my fault that my stepdad would body shame me as a child, (which indirectly created huge insecurities and a poor relationship with food for me as a young adult), nor was it my fault that he stopped me taking any belongings from the family home when I moved out at 16 years old, the reality is that by identifying my ghosts, allowing myself to sit with the pain, and get comfortable feeling uncomfortable about the facts, I was finally able to lay my ghosts to rest. Interestingly, the part that got the most airtime in therapy for me, was the feeling of inadequacy and abandonment when my stepdad decided to cut me out of his life completely by the time I was 24 years old.

He had created a whole new family through infidelity, without my mother's knowledge and then decided it would be easier to close the door and pretend I didn't exist. Having sat with that pain for many years, I now know that my stepdad's actions were the actions of a vulnerable man. A man so consumed in his own pain and his own ghosts, that he didn't realise, or intentionally know he was creating some huge ones for me. He was a classic avoidant and when you got close, he would pull away. Correction, he would run away.

The reality is, it really isn't and shouldn't be about blame or fault when addressing our ghosts. My body insecurities and lack of trust for men may have sadly started with him, but what continued was ultimately a lack of self-care, self-love, and self-belief, so that must be on me, surely. Remember, we have a choice, I just held that mirror up later than I should.

It's crazy to look back and see yourself with the same pair of eyes, but with more clarity. I guess it goes back to my point around self-care and inheriting 20:20 vision.

I spent years blaming my stepdad for my hurt, my sadness, and my inability to connect and trust other men, but the truth is, whilst he may have created those initial wounds, how deep and how raw they continued to get, really was and is my responsibility.

You must choose to stop letting history control your present and be comfortable enough to label your ghosts, to help move forward rather than backwards. To that end, it was strange to witness history repeating itself, with my attachment style becoming more anxious.

The penny dropped and I realised, astonishingly, I had spent years being drawn to avoidant men. I can now see, I wanted to be the fixer, the problem solver and was clearly searching for acceptance in all the wrong places. When I read that back, it's crazy to think I'm writing about myself. It's almost like I'm referring to a completely different woman, and to a point, I guess I am. Back then, I wasn't willing to be truly vulnerable and I wasn't courageous enough to sit in the pain until my early 30s.

When I finally labelled my ghosts in therapy, it was in that very moment, that I started to heal. As with every great book, our life has a beginning, a middle and an end. Arguably the beginning and end are the chapters we have very little control over.

The middle, however, is gold dust, the sweet spot, the sphere of control. It's our present and it's right here in the present we get the opportunity to turn the page and start a new chapter. One with full control! The hardest part is giving yourself permission to make those decisions and to show yourself and others what vulnerability looks like, with no shame.

By labelling your ghost, you get to show up baring those wounds from your past. The difference being, the narrative in your head and the voice that speaks up, is coming from the strong person in your present. The one that shines unapologetically!

Step 3 Practice Self ♡ Care

Knowing when you're vulnerable and why, is half the battle. The real work, however, comes into play when you are willing to commit to ongoing self-care. Self-care means taking the time to do things that help you live well and improve both your physical health and mental health. The gift of time, kindness, and forgiveness to yourself, naturally become essential ingredients and prevent us from defaulting to drama over peace.

The drama triangle theory was developed by Stephen Karpman in 1960 and is an invaluable tool to help increase your self-awareness and self-management around emotional triggers.

The simplicity of knowing we all at some point will find ourselves in a drama triangle, makes so much sense and again, an example whereby labels can be a positive thing, to if nothing more, educate ourselves.

There are many versions of the drama triangle, however much like any typical movie on Netflix, the roles can be defined as 'hero, villain, and victim'. There's a good chance you will unknowingly find yourself dancing in all three corners of the triangle, which can have catastrophic implications to your professional career and personal relationships. The Good news is we can all break from 'the drama' and enter an empowerment dynamic whereby we are more self-aware, vulnerable and outcome focused.

You ultimately need to start to create more positive habits and be able to identify if you're operating above or below the line in every aspect of your life, especially leadership and love.

Making a conscious move to operate your life from above the line, where there is oxygen in the air, where you can creatively challenge, be comfortable showing vulnerability and install a consistent growth mind-set is extremely liberating.

Imagine seeing yourself through a different lens. A lens that enables you to offer kindness, a lens that gives you the courage to label your ghost when it turns up completely uninvited. Helping you step away from the drama and stop letting your history manifest itself in your present. Believe me when I say, you don't need to imagine, it's 100% possible. You just need to be willing to hold the mirror up, stop self-sabotaging and be willing to offer unconditional kindness to the person that needs it the most. YOU! A non-negotiable part of the healing process that gets you a step closer to being your authentic self.

The Power of Pause

So, imagine. You've lifted the bonnet; you're now starting to understand yourself and your triggers. You've identified your ghosts and you're now practicing self-care. The question is, does that now mean those ghosts will completely disappear? Sadly not! That's wishful thinking. The truth is, they will always be lingering in the background and will always make you feel vulnerable.

However, don't forget, knowledge is power and accepting they will always be in the shadows, coupled with the reassurance that you can now comfortably manage them, should be enough. You can choose to live in the light and this self-investment journey will provide you with facts and coping mechanisms.

Having the power to be less reactive when triggered is the secret to moving from fear to freedom.

This is where the power of pause could make all the difference.

Remember:

- Know your triggers
- Label you ghost
- Be kind to yourself by pressing pause

Take a breath to process how you're feeling and why.

- Listen to your heart and don't forget, your ghost of the past doesn't define who you are.

Exercise

Time to Reflect

What do you believe your attachment style is and why?

....

....

....

....

....

....

What/who emotionally triggers you?

....

....

....

....

....

What/ who is your ghost of the past, and how does it impact you?

....

....

....

....

....

Chapter 3
You are What You Value

Aligning Your Behaviours
with Your Values

"You Don't Become What You Want, You Become What You Believe."

Oprah Winfrey

At 39 years old, I found myself in familiar territory. Divorce was on the horizon, for the second time. The funny thing is, when you remove 'judgment' from both your internal critic and that inflicted by others, divorce is ultimately a piece of paper, right?

You've probably heard that saying, unlucky in love, and this is usually expressed about a person that struggles to stay in a long-term relationship, through no fault of their own.

So, when you think about it, divorce is essentially, a relationship between two people that simply didn't work out. Nothing more, nothing less! That said, like many milestones in life, we're forced into a state of vulnerability and find ourselves, temporarily dancing with that feeling of disappointment. And let's face it, the feeling of disappointment, especially in ourselves, is the absolute worst.

When I think back to younger Charmaine, it's crazy how my outlook on relationships and love were completely different. That hopeless romantic in me believed that there was one person out there for everyone. One true love, soul mate even, and for me, I believed I had to go on a journey to find that person.

Weirdly the emphasis was always on this idealist man. Who they were, and what they could bring to me. Not once did I think of me, and what value I brought to a relationship. Shocking really, to think I would contemplate a future with such little care or consideration to my own value, worth and needs.

I now see things very differently. Is there only one person for everyone? Is love alone, enough? In my opinion, 100% not! Okay, this may sound bitter and slightly cynical, but what I'm simply saying is, love alone can't possibly create a long lasting, healthy relationship. You need alignment of values, vision, and lifestyle to compliment that big heart shaped L bomb. Only then can it truly flourish.

It's the same with leadership. You may outwardly express love for your job and what you do, however, if the company you work for doesn't share the same values, or the same vision, or your vision and values aren't respected, and your lifestyle needs aren't met. The chances are, there will be a shelf life applied to your position and it's only a matter of time before you start to seek fulfilment elsewhere. I guess you could say age and life experience has something to do with this profound viewpoint.

The reality is, I was born in the early 80s and was a child of the 90s; it's fair to say emotions, vulnerability and values were never really discussed growing up. I was one of three girls fighting for attention back then, and if I displayed emotion or expressed my feelings, they would very quickly be dismissed. I'd be labelled as a 'drama queen' or 'over sensitive'. I absolutely get that parents back then didn't intentionally dismiss their children's vulnerability; they just didn't have the platform to grant themselves and others permission to express themselves without judgment.

Being vulnerable or displaying vulnerability would be seen as a weakness and values, well, how on earth can your behaviours align with your values if you're unable to show up authentically in the first place.

I've spent a huge chunk of my adult life being unapologetic about my values and have genuinely worn them like a badge of honour, both personally and professionally, but here's the thing. Whilst I've always endeavoured to live by my values, it's only been in recent years that I realised the impact my behaviours, and the alignment with others and their values, has had on me, both in leadership and in love. So, you're probably now thinking; what does alignment of values have to do with divorce? Surprisingly, so much!

Divorce the second time round was hugely different for me. My first husband was a gentleman, he was smart, caring, he was a man that had strong morals and values. We fell out of love and realised the vision and lifestyle we both desired, were somewhat different. Even though our relationship broke down, we respected each other. We both displayed a level of honesty and kindness to one another. No legal advice was needed, and we maintained a healthy level of communication.

We even remained friends for a period after separation and would meet for dinner to check in and see how each other was.

I remember feeling so lucky and grateful that we could close our relationship chapter with such dignity. This was circa 16 years ago and when I talk about those light bulb moments, this was one of them.

Whilst we fell out of love, wanted different things, and had a different vision for the future, our values were similar. We were honest, respectful, caring, and transparent. The truth is, our values come with a set of behaviours, some we're aware of and some we are not.

Normally our values are consistent in all aspects of our lives. They are you; they are your core and subconsciously you're driven by them, and you respond and behave differently because of them.

Let me give you an example. Most of us will be able to recall a time when we felt enormously upset because someone didn't act on something they implicitly said they would do. So, the question is, why would someone else, choosing not to deliver against expectations that they verbally set out for themselves, bother us so much?

Whilst not always recognised or said out loud, we will deem this as violation of one of our own 'personal values'.

While sometimes our rules are indeed valid, other times they are just plain silly. We are all unique and driven by different values and expectations. The set of personal values we hold, will dictate how we interact with and judge other people. Some of us show frustration outwardly, whilst others internalise this upset, and hold grudges.

Our values also dictate how we view ourselves and how we see the world. We carry bugbears and a perceived concept of how things 'should' be. This is turn can then impact how we show up as a leader and lover.

Think about it: when you say or hear things like, 'If you loved me, you wouldn't do 'XY & Z'. A rule or value that we expect the people around us to follow. We often impose our values on people around us, without telling them about our expectations or needs, which only results in disappointment and frustration. Put simply, your values drive your behaviour, and your behaviour drives the outcome (be it right or wrong).

Your values and those of your colleagues, friends and family will have a direct impact on the quality of your relationships, so it's important to not only understand your own but also those you're closest to you.

Good leadership requires the ability to communicate, motivate and delegate, sometimes simultaneously requiring you to forge ahead without all the answers. For the control freaks out there, this alone will make you vulnerable.

Whilst I've spent many years practicing self-care, self-love, and kindness to myself, it's fair to say that being faced with divorce for the second time made me feel the most vulnerable I've ever felt. The internal narrative in my head was saying that I'd failed at love and marriage, and I'd let my family down. I knew I was being honest. I knew my vision for the future didn't feature that of a man that made me feel sad and dulled my light, and I knew the life I wanted to create for my daughter's future, required me to be authentic, real, happy, and sincere.

The reality is, you can make bold, brave decisions, that are fundamentally the right one's for you and those around you. However, in doing so, you have to be prepared to stare vulnerability in the face, to have difficult conversations, to face forward, to be courageous and believe that whilst the road ahead is rocky, the sun will always rise on a new day and you will be a step closer to being authentically you, with no apologies. Being true to yourself is fundamental to your growth. It's not about following the status quo; it's about leading from the front and with your heart.

Divorce number two wasn't easy. I was with my now ex-husband, for 9 years and our beautiful daughter Florence was born before we even reached our two-year anniversary. Things moved quickly, they were unplanned, so unsurprisingly values, vision and lifestyle evidently took a back seat.

What's clear now is our misalignments on values and vision, contributed to what was a very turbulent relationship. I didn't realise the link with values and behaviours then but having spent the time to lift the bonnet and being presented with the cold hard facts, it's almost impossible to ignore.

It's important to differentiate between aspirational values and actual values. So many people will claim that 'honesty' is a core value, that 'kindness' is a core value, but if their behaviours are not aligned and ultimately tell a different story, the chances are, they are telling the world what they think they want to hear. What is expected! What they think 'good' looks like. But that mask will 100% slip at some point.

Honesty is a core value of mine. Okay, I'm human, so it's fair to say there have been moments in my life I didn't speak up immediately. Moments when I recognised the truth would be hard for others to hear and accept. But I'm proud that I would always eventually speak my truth because the alternative was never an option.

I would communicate with my ex-husband when I was feeling unhappy, when things were upsetting me and when I requested something different from him.

He was a classic bury his head in the sand type of guy, he would see life through rose tinted glasses, fear change and eventually resented me for being honest regularly about my feelings. He disliked how I would articulate my truth and rather than hold the mirror up himself, he would shout at me because of his internal frustration and evident inability to face his demands and show up authentically. Unsurprisingly, he would regularly trigger my 'ghost of the past' and his lack of honesty with himself about our fundamental differences caused me a lot of stress.

It got to a point of such extreme pain and vulnerability, that I would barely recognise myself. My actions and behaviour shifted. I would be drawn into regular disagreements and negative conversations.

I was honest and he didn't want to hear the truth. Our values and behaviours weren't aligned and rather than accepting our differences, the relationship became more and more toxic, and respect was lost on both sides.

I didn't like the person I was with him and, separation was the only way forward to find some peace and provide a permanent platform to be our authentic selves without the heartache.

Living by our values means that we do more than profess our values, we practice them.

We walk our talk.

We're crystal clear about what we believe and hold important, and we ensure our intentions, thoughts, words, and behaviours align with those beliefs.

5 steps to aligning your behaviours to your values and showing up authentically:

- View the list of core values below and start to understand what sits at the core of you.
- Articulate your values to others and explain why they are so important.
- Learn the values of those you lead and love and understand where there may be differences.
- Understand the behaviours that show up, attached to your values and those around you.
- Encourage others to go on this journey with you.

•Authenticity	•Friendships	•Peace
•Achievement	•Fun	•Pleasure
•Adventure	•Growth	•Poise
•Authority	•Happiness	•Popularity
•Autonomy	•Honesty	•Recognition
•Balance	•Humour	•Religion
•Beauty	•Influence	•Reputation
•Boldness	•Inner Harmony	•Respect
•Compassion	•Justice	•Responsibility
•Challenge	•Kindness	•Security
•Citizenship	•Knowledge	•Self-Respect
•Community	•Leadership	•Service
•Competency	•Learning	•Sensitivity
•Contribution	•Love	•Stability
•Creativity	•Loyalty	•Success
•Curiosity	•Meaningful Work	•Status
•Determination	•Openness	•Trustworthiness
•Fairness	•Optimism	•Wealth
•Faith		•Wisdom

Exercise:

You are what you value!

What would you define as your core values & why?

....
....
....
....

How do your values effect your behaviour and actions?

....
....
....
....

What values do you look for in a partner?

....
....
....
....

What Values do you look for in a leader?

....
....
....
....

Know your worth, not just your values!

Okay, so you now know your core values, you know the behaviours that could potentially show up in support of these and you're now starting to learn about others and the role your values foster in personal and professional relationships. The question is, do you know your worth?

Feels like a crazy question, I know. But do you know your true worth?

Do you back yourself 100%? And do you know what red flags might look like in others? The type of red flag that could take you to that vulnerability crossroad of self-belief or self-loathing?

Someone once told me, it's so important to separate how you feel about someone, from how someone makes you feel. The two things are fundamentally different and can apply to a workplace, leader, situation, or partner. For example, you could feel someone is charismatic, courageous, fun, smart etc. but if they make you feel lonely, sad, inadequate, anxious, and have you questioning your value, then *that,* right there, is the reality of your relationship. So, you can think someone is a god, that your boss has a great reputation, your friend is popular, the workplace environment is award winning. The truth is, if they make you feel like you're nothing, then that will be your experience.

Returning to the world of dating in my late 30s, really opened my eyes. Knowing that you've had years of therapy to support your self-development journey, believing in yourself, your worth and what you value is something that shouldn't be taken for granted.

There will always be bumps in the road. Sadly, people will want to make you question your worth and your value. But it's in these very moments we need to immediately hold the mirror up and be strong enough to step away from relationships that don't embrace you, and your authentic glory.

We are all unique, our stories are unique, and our career ladders and relationship will always be very different. So, own your values, know your worth and proudly take a step forward.

Great things happen when we step out of our comfort zone and take a leap of faith in ourselves.

- Be your own biggest fan.
- Love yourself.
- Gift yourself the things you need.

It's a non-negotiable investment, believe me.

Chapter 4
Goal Setting with Your Heart

Chasing Feelings, Not Numbers

"Setting Goals is the First Step in Turning the Invisible into the Visible."

Tony Robbins

It was the middle of April 2015. My daughter was born two weeks earlier, and as she lay in her mosses basket, taking a nap, I remember sat in the bay window of my 2-bedroom Victorian terraced house, with the sun beaming on my face, thinking, *How can I provide unconditional love for this tiny human I've created.*

I remember that moment, like it was yesterday. I remember all the details, how she looked while she was sleeping, what I was wearing, even how the sun beaming through the venetian blinds, created shadow lines on the cuddle chair I sat on.

I was a new mother, so naturally I was sleep deprived and tired. But in that moment, I felt strangely awake, hugely present, and curious about the future.

I started to think about what my daughter might look like when she grows up, who she will be, what she will value, the type of school she will attend and then, I thought about where we might end up living. It's funny, because my initial primary thought was how I could provide unconditional love for Florence, but very quickly, my brain turned to stability and material things.

Our job as a parent is to nurture, love, support and yes, provide. As I looked around the room, whilst I felt a huge sense of pride that I owned the house my daughter lay asleep in, astonishingly, in the blink of an eye, it felt redundant. I started to think about what a 'family home' would now look like to me and most importantly, why. I sat there and closed my eyes and visioned a house. It was white in colour, detached, with gates and had a big garden. The mind is such a powerful tool; I started thinking about my next big goal. I wanted to buy that detached white house. I wanted to be successful enough to buy that family home and give my daughter roots, safety, stability and above all, I wanted somewhere that she could create positive childhood memories. Of course, my head was now swamped with numbers and before long I was on right move furiously looking for that detached white house, to give me an indication of how hard I'd need to work and how I could achieve that goal.

Interestingly, I now know why it was so important to me. It wasn't to post on social media, nor was it to brag to others that I was going up in the world; it was simply because I wanted to give my daughter a platform for happy memories. Maybe my lack of happy childhood memories or my inability to remember them, contributed towards that vision.

Now wait, I absolutely know that a house can't possibly replace love, but I equally recognise that we would have survived without it. But "wow," I thought in that moment. It would be such a gift to provide, what in my mind were, the foundations for beautiful memories. The seed in the garden of childhood happiness if you like! I immediately knew, I had to make this goal, dream even, a reality.

I recently read that when there is harmony between our mind, heart and resolution, nothing is impossible. A statement I believe to be true. It's fair to say that most of us have an image in our head of what an ideal life, relationship or job might look like. We normally know what we want to achieve. Even without the noise of external influences, certain goals seem to captivate us. We turn into magpies and are attracted to the shiny stuff. We design our lives around achieving these ideals because we think they will make us happy. But the million-dollar question is, will they make us happy?

Do we even know how to measure how we feel, and do we set goals because we think we should or because they will bring us genuine fulfilment?

Material gratification is external, but happiness is very much internal.

Fast forward to July 2017, I got the keys to a four-bedroom detached house, white in colour, electric gates, and large garden. I watched my two-year-old daughter walk through the front door smiling, ready to explore her new home. I felt elated, proud, happy, emotional, fulfilled. All the feelings were at the surface, and I was proud that two years on from setting myself a goal, that was absolutely driven by my heart, I managed to make it a reality, I achieved it, all by myself and my god, that felt so good.

I mention the white detached house, not to create unrealistic, ideological views of what a family home should look like. Clearly, we all recognise it's the feeling that means more. It's because I now know that not every milestone we achieve in life, provides that same level of fulfilment. It's so unbelievably confusing and demotivating to reach, what you think was once an impossible dream. That type of goal, that would feel like all your Christmas's had come at once, or fireworks going off on New Year's Eve! To then be left feeling, well, completely numb, absolutely nothing at all. Let me say that again, you achieve that big goal and there are no fireworks, there are no feelings, you feel nothing. If anything, you feel sad.

Had someone told me this, when I set up my business, I wouldn't have believed them at all. It would have made zero sense. I guess it comes back to those light bulb moments in life, and it was only a few years ago I realised how unsatisfying it was to achieve big financial milestones. Ultimately, achieving smart goals when heart or purpose aren't in the driving seat.

What does that even mean? I mean, we spend our lives striving for bigger and better, and the sad reality is, so many of us unknowingly live in a state of glass half empty and consume ourselves with thoughts around what we don't have, as opposed to what we do. On reflection, many of my goals over the years where set from a head strong, businesswoman that wanted to achieve the equivalent status of others as opposed to setting meaningful goals with my heart. That's crazy, right? I'm an empath for goodness' sake. I nurture, I care, I'm proud to be different. But somehow, at different stages, I inevitably fell into the comparison trap and ending up chasing the numbers, not the feeling.

Any goal set with heart and purpose was guaranteed to land every single time with me, it felt bloody fantastic. Watching a member of staff buy their first house, have their first child, raising over £45,000 for Cancer Research UK, giving my daughter a platform for childhood memories, taking my best friend away to Barcelona to show her how much I valued her, building a cabin in my daughter's school to support vulnerable children. All these goals were driven and executed with my heart, and fulfilment was inevitable.

On the flip side, earning over £100K, over £250K, achieving millionaire status, watching £1m turnover become £2m, then £5m, then £10m, then £20m. I mean, the number only continues to rise and sadly the feeling decreases. There's zero emotion behind them, they are just numbers.

These were goals set with my head because I thought it was the logical next step. Aspirational financial goals that I believed every business owner should want to achieve. I confused growth mind-set with numbers growing and believe me, there's a difference. Watching numbers grow was making me feel empty and I genuinely thought there was something wrong with me.

When you think about it, there's no real surprise here, of course I felt empty, they weren't aligned with me, my values, or my heart. It's almost crazy to expect fulfilment and fireworks from what is ultimately an empty goal. I have a motto in life. No good can come from staring out the window, the answer will always lay within. What I'm saying is comparison, genuinely is the thief of all joy. Okay, of course money lends to material things, quality of life and we all like nice things. But the cold hard facts are, a goal should be set by you, for you, and it should be smart, but led by the heart.

Only then, will you reach your true, sustainable version of fulfilment.

SMART + HEART = FULFILMEN

I'll give you an example. That detached white house with electric gates and a big garden. It was my dream, my goal. It had a financial target, a measurable realistic time frame to achieve it and it had 100% heart. It meant something to me, and the heart part of that goal became my core driver. I was left fulfilled. But imagine if the purchase of that home wasn't driven by my heart? Let's assume, it was for status, to show the world I could afford it, and was ultimately a representation of my financial success. Zero heart whatsoever. You know what's coming. I would have felt nothing. Yes, okay, it's a nice house. But get the keys, pop the champagne, move in and then what? Find yourself on right move again, looking for the next BIG house. You'd inevitably keep chasing bigger and better. It has no meaning or purpose, and this results in no feeling.

SMART goals, as we call them in the business world, are quantitative in nature. They're specific, measurable, attainable, relevant and time based. They ultimately allow us to measure progress and success easily, with numbers, facts and figures. When delivered, these goals encourage us to create more aggressive goals. When not met, they reveal problems in our process which drive us to make changes and get back on track.

SMART goals have many great qualities, but they're lacking heart and soul. That's the problem and the route course to that empty feeling. So, setting a goal based solely on a number isn't enough. In some cases, it's impossible, because many truly meaningful heart goals can't be measured with facts and figures.

I guess the big question is, how can we set goals that have a healthy balance of smart and heart? The below shows that you can retain some of the fundamentals of a smart model but ultimately forces you to lift the bonnet emotionally around how you want to feel and why a goal is important to you.

Connecting with the core and acknowledging your feelings or lack of feelings might just change your approach and mind-set when setting goals with your heart, not just your head.

Now, think about a new goal and fill in the below exercise using the heart model. Ask yourself the questions below and reflect on what this goal means to you. Remember your emotions will be your driving force so really spend the time to think about this.

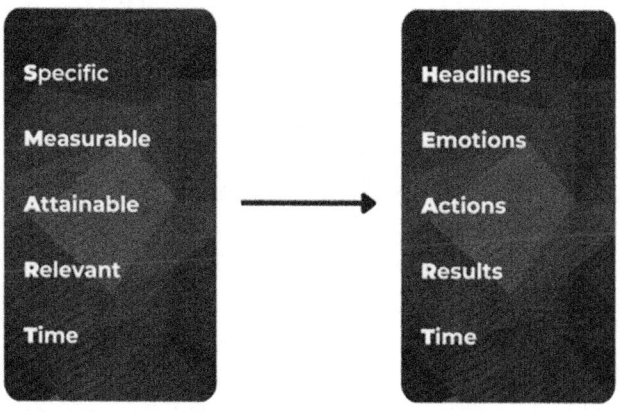

Exercise

Goal Setting with Your Heart

Headlines

Q: What is the headline goal/ financials/ numbers that you want to achieve?

....

....

Emotions

Q: How do you want to feel when achieved, what feeling are you chasing? / What does this mean to present/future you/others?

....

....

Actions

Q: What massive actions/ changes do you need to take to achieve this goal? Are they realistic?

....

....

Results

Q: How will you know the goal has been achieved? What does success look/feel like?

....

....

Time

Q: How much time needs to be dedicated to achieving this goal? / When could it be achieved?

....

....

To be clear, this isn't to say you can't also have SMART goals, but I challenge and encourage you to attach a feeling, through using the HEART model.

The reality is, the less pure your goals are, the less likely they are to make us happy and provide fulfilment.

I remember reading an extract from Brene Brown that really struck a chord with me. She said that when it comes to vulnerability, it's the first thing we look for in others and the last thing we want others to see in ourselves. This will resonate with so many people. There's clearly a misalignment here and 100% comes back to fear.

During this journey so far, you've held the mirror up, acknowledged how your past can spill into your present, you're starting to understand who you are, what you value and most importantly given yourself permission to be vulnerable and show up authentically.

Goal setting with your heart, knowing how you want to feel and giving your heart permission to lead, will ultimately shape your future and provide you the confidence to wear that cape. You can show up as your true, authentic, vulnerable, self. The hard work is done, you now need to be willing to take the hand of your inner child and lead the way to that final door of discovery. Anything is possible if you believe.

Chapter 5
Owning Your New Superpowers!

Cut the Cord and Wear the Cape

"When We Have the Courage to Walk into Our Own Story and Own It, We Get to Write the Ending."
Brene Brown

It was the 5th of July 2023; the time was 12.15pm and suddenly there was a knock at the door. I hear those dreaded words, "The judge is ready for you now." It's strange because I've felt vulnerable, many times in my life, but today was different. Some 14 months on from an emotional roller-coaster of a battle with my ex-husband, and for the first time ever, I felt exposed. I felt zero control and most of all, I felt overwhelmingly vulnerable. It's hard for me to articulate why in that moment, things were so different. There were physical changes in me. My mouth was dry, my hands visibly shaking. Tears were falling uncontrollably down my cheeks, and I had an ache in my chest, like my heart was breaking.

I felt all the emotions; anxiety, sadness, disappointment, fear, anger. I thought how an earth was someone like me, standing in a court room. What I mean by this, is, me, a woman that has spent her entire life putting everyone else first, someone that cares so much about making a difference and empowering other people to become the best version of themselves finds herself in court. Being judged, analysed, vulnerability oozing from me and ultimately feeling like a stranger in my own body. As dramatic as it sounds, I felt like a criminal being sentenced.

You see, I'm the kind of person that celebrates difference, someone that finds the gift in literally everything. Probably to the point of annoyance for some of my staff, friends, and family. So, when faced with someone displaying the opposite of my values, I mean, the worst type of dishonesty, the type being used, to leverage financially gain, it's fair to say, that reality check hit me so hard in the face, literally like a ton of bricks. I always offer trust, so willingly and so freely and I guess, just live in hope that others will gift me the same level of kindness, that I unconditionally offer them. I now know, life isn't always like this.

We can't control how others behave and that's sometimes a bitter pill to swallow, but equally an important lesson to learn.

When you think about how many wasted hours, days, years even, some of us have anguished over, when fuelled with negative energy and thoughts surrounding the actions inflicted by someone else, when so wildly out of our sphere of control, we still let it consume us. Define us. And effectively give permission to the feeling of vulnerability, with zero control, solution, or positive outcome. Let me say that again. We accept the feeling of vulnerability with no solution or positive outcome. It's outrageously frightening to think, that most of us find ourselves defaulting here. Now, what if I told you that we all have our own pair of metaphoric scissors? Furthermore, what if I told you that we have the power to cut the cord of control at any time? We can break free from a person, situation or environment that holds us prisoner. There's no user manual needed, just a little bit of self-love and courage to believe that freedom is possible.

With that comes a level of acceptance, that there will be a grieving process that follows this. But that's okay and hopefully now, you know, It's 100% okay to feel vulnerable when processing how you reached that point of freedom. When talking to my therapist about such feelings, she thankfully reminded me that certain people or situations will always trigger me but every time we face a new challenge, those scissors will be sharper and my ability to cut the cord will get easier and quicker.

As I watched a chapter of my life play out in front of my eyes, with minimal control on the outcome, it genuinely took my breath away. As a strong female entrepreneur that has spent a decade in business empowering others to show up authentically and not fear vulnerability, I had to acknowledge, that for now, my voice had been silenced, and no one was listening.

Vulnerability is so complex. Control plays a huge factor in comfort ability. What I mean by that, is, if you feel vulnerable, but you're fully in control of 'what next' and how you move forward, the chances are, you find a way to get comfortable with being uncomfortable. However, if you find yourself feeling vulnerable at the hands of someone else, and forced to relinquish control of the outcome, and rely on someone else to dictate what that next chapter in your life might look like. My God! It's the most debilitating, uncomfortable, heart wrenching feeling. I simply wasn't prepared for the injustice that day. The road to acceptance and showing up as your authentic self, time and time again despite the bumps in the road, is a long one. It's on-going, it always needs work, and will always be challenging. But the short-term pain is absolutely worth the long-term gain, as cliché as it sounds.

We can't change the mind-set of others or the pain they choose to inflict, but we can control who we are.

We can control what we stand for, and we can turn that page and know that next chapter will be one full of grit, resilience, and a ridiculous amount of heart.

As I left the court room, I headed straight to the ladies bathroom to take a minute and splash my flustered face with cold water. I stopped and starred at my reflection in the mirror. I knew the only way to get through the day was to remind myself how blessed I was. I couldn't let this moment in time, define my future.

It got me thinking about another light bulb moment my therapist had gifted me with a few years before.

"Charmaine, close your eyes," she said.

"Now imagine you're walking down the street in your new fur coat (faux, not real of course.)

"You step outside the door.

"The wind is in your hair, sunshine on your face. You take a few steps out, onto a busy High-street and start walking.

"People start to turn and stare at you and your beautiful new coat. The question is, does the fur coat wear you or do you wear the coat?"

Lift the bonnet on this, her laboured point here was: When you show up, is your head held high and are you owning who you really are? Are you proud?

Are you removing judgment on yourself and loving the whole person inside that coat? It's a big question, and just saying these words out loud enables you to change the ending to your story. The truth is, that coat was absolutely wearing me when I entered that court room. But by the time I reached the ladies bathroom, held the mirror up and realised that whatever the outcome, I would be okay, I was able to readjust my coat. I wiped my tears and said the words "I AM WEARING THE COAT".

As the door swung open, I left the bathroom a different woman. I knew, I was now wearing my coat with pride, and I wouldn't let anyone take my shine. I chose to move from the shadow into the light. It's possible for us to feel 100% vulnerable, but also know that when we hold the mirror up, we love what we see.

When you reflect on how you've been described by others over the years, it's quite fascinating to think how those uninvited comments/words, have potentially impacted you. For me, some have made me smile, made me proud, whilst others have made me feel sad, extremely vulnerable and in some cases, stopped me from showing up authentically in fear of being judged. Chief juggler, the guru, the therapist, the clown, the mother, the ice queen, boss bitch, big balls, emotional woman, to name a few.

But there's one that whilst initially I didn't accept, I now see differently. 'Superwoman'. I mean, take the superhero quality out of it, and look at the words, Super, woman. I used to live with Imposter Syndrome and not see the incredible woman staring back at me. I used to hate my body, question my leadership skills, my parenting skills and I'd sadly question whether I deserved love because of my adolescent abandonment issues. I now proudly walk down the street with my head held high, and smile. I know I'm worthy, I know I'm good person and I know I enrich other people's lives. I've moved out of the queue of self-doubt and that feels bloody fantastic.

We all have battle wounds, and those wounds won't always be so raw. They stop hurting as much and ultimately turn into a scar. Some days we don't notice those scars, when other days, that scar itches, becomes inflamed and we may just find ourselves transported back to a time that wound was fresh and painful. Remember, in that moment, you need to grab your cape from the wardrobe and place it round your neck.

You must change the dialogue in your own brain and get out of your own way. Remember, "hate" has four letters but so does "love". "Enemies" has seven letters, but so does "friends". "Lying" has five letters but so does "truth". "Cry" has three letters but so does "joy". "Negativity" has 10 letters but so does "positivity". Life is two sided, much like a coin. The difference is, we have full control over which side that coin lands. The element of chance can absolutely be removed. There must be commitment to empower ourselves daily and commitment to want to choose the better side.

To be clear, being positive doesn't mean you're visibly happy all the time, that's simply not realistic. Being positive means when you face a challenge or an obstacle, try to know that everything happens for a reason. Even if, in that very moment, you're not entirely sure what it is. Once you've overcome that challenge, and believe me when I say, you always will. We learn a valuable lesson. And it's right here, in that lesson, that we grow. We blossom and truly Flourish.

Imagine tomorrow you turn the page and its day 1. Day 1 of you showing up authentically, vulnerably, and unapologetically. What ultimately needs to change for this to happen?

Exercise

What changes need to happen in your life, to ensure you show up authentically, vulnerably, and unapologetically on day 1?

....
....
....
....
....
....
....

What element of control do you have to cut the cord on?

....
....
....
....
....
....

What does your vulnerability cape look like and how does it make you feel?

....
....
....
....
....
....

We get one shot at this thing called life, and if we want to live a happy, fulfilled one, we must armour up and know that some of the chapters in our book would not be there through choice. However, you are who you are today because of them. Because most of us have worked insanely hard to remove the judgment, the stigma, the barriers, the perception, etc.

Our stories are unique, as is our pain. For that reason, comparison is the thief of all joy. We need to own our story, own our scars, and know that being vulnerable is your ultimate superpower. When you're vulnerable, you build empathy. We can let down our walls and develop the art of articulating our feelings. When we understand ourselves fully, we become equipped to understand others. This helps us become better leaders, lovers, parents, and friends.

We can accept that forgiveness is a critical part of the healing process and become willing to offer our full heart to others without worrying that history will repeat itself.

We can choose to show up authentically and understand that in those moments of vulnerability, a new lesson is discovered, a new string to our bow is added and a new chapter is born. A chapter where we face forward with more curiosity and less fear.

So, in the words of Martin Luther King;

Take the first step in faith. You don't have to see the whole staircase, just the first step.

Be proud of your journey so far and start getting excited about what tomorrow will bring.

Be courageous.

Be authentic.

Be vulnerable.

BE YOU, with NO apologies!

Printed in Great Britain
by Amazon

56117813R00046